T0065373

C.R.A.S.H. COURSE

A Foundation for the Christian in College

Quinton Englebright &
Haylee Holeman

WESTBOW
PRESS®
A DIVISION OF THOMAS NELSON
& ZONDERVAN

WestBow Press books may be ordered through booksellers or by contacting:

WestBow Press
A Division of Thomas Nelson & Zondervan
1663 Liberty Drive
Bloomington, IN 47403
www.westbowpress.com
844-714-3454

ISBN: 978-1-6642-2255-7 (sc)
ISBN: 978-1-6642-2254-0 (e)

Print information available on the last page.

WestBow Press rev. date: 02/11/2021

ABOUT THE AUTHOR

Quinton is currently pursuing a Master of Christian Education at New Orleans Baptist Theological Seminary. He serves as an intern for NOLA Metro BCM as the leader for Leavell College BCM. He is married to Rebecca and they both graduated from the University of West Florida in Pensacola. He enjoys being on the water, good food, and traveling alongside Rebecca. His personal mission is for students to have a transformational engagement with Christ, be prepared to serve the Church, and to live for God's glory.

Haylee is currently pursuing a Master of Divinity at New Orleans Baptist Theological Seminary and hope to graduate in May 2022. She graduated from Mississippi college in May 2019, with a Bachelor of Arts in English. She is also a third-culture kid who grew up traveling between the U.S., Peru, and Mexico. It's safe to say that she loves to travel, and a lot of her personal writing has to do with exploring other cultures because that's where her heart belongs. She is a Captain America fanatic, a taco snob, and a Slytherin. But most importantly, she is a follower of Jesus, and she believes that He gave her the gift of words so that she can use them to further His kingdom here on earth.

CONTENTS

INTRODUCTION

"Stop your fighting, and know that I am God, exalted
among the nations, exalted on the earth."
Psalm 46:10

Before coming to college, I thought I knew what I wanted to do
in life. I had just gone through a difficult time in my life, and
I wanted to devote my life to Christ and stop living for myself.
My plan was to be a missionary while working as an engineer so
that I could have money while serving God. However, God had
other plans. In this section, I hope to show how God used my
college years to equip me in ministry and how the idea of Crash
Course came to be.

At the beginning of my college career, I joined extracurricular
activities, intramurals, and clubs that went with my major. A
friend from my home church in Crestview suggested that I join
Baptist Collegiate Ministries (BCM) because it was a Christian
group. I went to their weekly meeting, CRASH, and it was very
different compared to the other Christian events I had been to;
honestly, it was kind of weird. The students were super friendly,
their director was an old man, and they genuinely cared about
Jesus. However, I did not wholeheartedly commit to BCM yet
because I wanted to see what other opportunities college had to
offer.

In the next semester, BCM went on a mission trip. I knew I

should go since missions was what I wanted to do in the future. We drove almost three hours from campus to do evangelism to college students in Panama City Beach during Spring Break (Party Central!). Anytime the director, Tony, drives for a trip he has someone sit in the front seat, affectionately known as the "hot seat," to keep him awake but also to have discussion. Since I was the new freshman in the group, I had the pleasure of sitting in the "hot seat" the whole time. Tony asked me question after question about my life, my family, future plans, and what God has done in my life. I didn't realize then how important this conversation would be in my life, but this time in the "hot seat" kickstarted a mentoring relationship with Tony.

As the semesters continued, I took on more roles and responsibilities in BCM and enjoyed every second of it; I quickly gained a passion to serve others and to help them grow in Christ. Not only was I serving in BCM, but I also served at my church by the joining greeting team for Sunday mornings and helping with the teaching for the college group.

Eventually, I hit a fork in my school career where I had to choose between continuing in engineering or serving in the leadership team in BCM due to scheduling issues. It was during this time that Tony and other mentors helped me discern my calling to ministry. I had been using engineering as a fallback in case ministry didn't work out, but Tony told me that if I am called to ministry then I do not need to have a backup plan because God will always provide.

After accepting my calling to ministry, I was given more opportunities not only serve but to lead. Leading really caused me to grow because I learned how to teach, orchestrate strategic teams, and mobilize students for the gospel. All of the learning and leading eventually led to an idea for developing leaders within BCM, Crash Course. I wanted to create a curriculum that would be a starting framework for their Christian walk.

The idea for Crash Course came out of me observing different churches and their membership classes. In the same way that a church teaches a membership class, once a student joins a ministry or leadership team, the idea is that they would have this resource as an initial framework to build a foundation and to use to equip others. This book is not comprehensive for each subject, but rather it is a starting point to guide you in the right direction. At the beginning of each chapter, you will see a scripture verse. We encourage you to memorize it because you will begin to establish that discipline. In addition, read the materials that follow in the chapter, and if you want to know more information check out the resources we provide at the end of each chapter. I hope that you find this book helpful for whatever stage of life you find yourself in, and I pray that this would ultimately glorify God. -Quinton Englebright

ONE

෴

Christianity

"The Son is the radiance of God's glory and the exact
expression of his nature, sustaining all things by his
powerful word. After making purification for sins, he
sat down at the right hand of the Majesty on high."
Hebrews 1:3

The first letter of CRASH Course stands for "Christianity."
But what exactly is Christianity? What do you think of when
you think about Christianity? Jesus? Law? The Bible? Church
buildings? While all of these are aspects of it, you won't completely
understand Christianity without looking at the entire picture. For
example, you can't fully comprehend the significance of sin and
the Fall if you don't know that God didn't create the world to be
this way. You won't fully understand the significance of Jesus if
you don't recognize how He relates to Israel. When you see the
Bible as one overarching narrative and not disconnected parts, it
will transform how you read Scripture. You'll see connections
that you previously overlooked, and in the end, when God
restores His people, this will excite you even more because you

will recognize what a miracle it is that God wants to dwell with us in the first place.

Christianity is centered on the Word of God, the Bible. The Bible consists of two testaments, sixty-six books, 1,189 chapters, and each word is divinely inspired to reveal the actions of God throughout history as well as His relationship with humanity. We chose to divide the narrative into seven parts for the sake of clarity, but it is truly one consistent record of God's actions throughout history. God created the world, but humans decided that we didn't need him. We rebelled against God, but He has consistently and continuously worked bring us back into a relationship with Him. He sent His only son to defeat death so that He could restore that perfect relationship that we had before we fell away from God.

Not only that, but He desires that all who believe in Him would share their faith with others. That is exactly what this CRASH Course study is designed to help you do. We want to help you understand what you believe so that you can share it with other students on your campus and live out God's purpose for your life during your college years. You can use this particular chapter as a roadmap to share your faith, and because we've separated it into sections, you have the option to share it as one big presentation or meet together for multiple weeks and go more in depth.

Creation

Genesis 1-2 tells the story of how God created the universe. In a span of seven days, He spoke and miraculously created all things out of nothing. As He created, He repeatedly declared that His creation was good. To top off His creation, God created man and woman, Adam and Eve. God created humanity in His own image, meaning we take on characteristics of God Himself and have special placement in His creation. In his book *Pursuit of God*,

A.W. Tozer writes, "Being made in His image, we have within us the capacity to know Him."[1] The fact that God created us in His own image means that we can have a personal relationship with Him. After He created them, God placed Adam and Eve into the Garden of Eden so that they could care for His creation and so He could have fellowship with them.

In the garden, God provided for all of Adam and Eve's needs, and every creature lived in perfect harmony with Him. However, God did place one stipulation on the garden. One tree in the middle of the garden was off limits: the tree of the knowledge of good and evil. God warned Adam and Eve that they would surely die if they ate of this tree. For a time, Adam and Eve obeyed God and enjoyed His presence and creation, but one day they faced temptation, and everything changed.

The Fall

One day while Eve was tending to the garden, a serpent approached her and began to question what God had told her. In Genesis 3, the serpent deceived Eve, causing her to doubt God's goodness. She broke the one commandment that God had given her, not to eat from the tree of the knowledge of good and evil, and Adam followed suit. They both rejected God's leadership and because of their disobedience, Death, sin, shame, and evil entered into the world.

Adam and Eve, knowing what they had done, attempted to hide themselves from God because they were ashamed of their disobedience. And yet, despite their best efforts, they couldn't hide from God, and He confronted them about what they had done. He cursed them and drove them out of the garden because they could no longer enjoy His presence. They would now face the consequences of their choices. Because of their sin, all of their descendants, including you and I, possess a sin nature, meaning we are infected with sin and separated from God at birth. Not only does sin affect humanity, but all of creation suffers from the effects of sin. War, hatred, racism, and unrest, are just a few examples of the brokenness that has permeated the world because of sin. This is why everyone on earth needs a Savior, and God has faithfully provided one through Jesus Christ.

The first instance of God's promise of a Savior comes immediately after Adam and Eve sinned. In Genesis 3:15, God promises a Savior who would crush the serpent's head, defeating him once and for all.

"I will put hostility between you and the woman,
and between your offspring and her offspring.
He will strike your head,
and you will strike his heel."

Despite man's disobedience, God still desired fellowship with them and promised to restore the perfect relationship once again.

Covenant

Over time, Adam and Eve had children and their children had more children, and they continued to reproduce and populate the earth. However, these children continued to disobey God and reject His leadership. One man stood out to God as righteous, and his name was Abram. In Genesis 12, God told Abram to leave his home and take his family to an unknown land that the Lord would show Him. Abram obeyed God, and he proved himself a faithful follower of God. Though Abram made many mistakes along the way, he continued to walk with God throughout his life. God saw his faith and promised to use his descendants to bless the whole world.

Despite the fact that Abram and his wife Sarai had served the

Lord and lived faithfully for Him, they never had any children of their own. In Genesis 15, God formed a covenant with Abram and revealed His plan to him. A covenant is like a promise or a contract. Numerous covenants come into play in Scripture, and this particular one between God and Abram is called the "Abrahamic Covenant." In the "Abrahamic Covenant," God promised that Abram's descendants would be as numerous as the stars in the sky. Not only that, but God told Abram that He would use Abram's descendants to bless the whole earth. Yet, Abram reached the age of ninety-nine and still had no children. God appeared to Abram again in Genesis 17 and reminded him of the covenant previously made, promising once again to multiply his descendants. God promised that kings and nations would come from Abram's descendants, and that they would dwell in the land of Canaan forever.

However, the greatest and most important part of this covenant was that God promised to always be the God of Abram's descendants. They would be His people, and He would always be with them. Not only that, but God revealed that all nations on earth would be blessed because of Abram's descendants. Today, we know that Jesus Christ came as a descendant of Abram, so what God was promising in this moment was that salvation for the whole world would come through Abram's family. To seal the deal and confirm the covenant, God changed the names of both Abram and Sarai to Abraham and Sarah. He also issued the mandate of circumcision, which would set apart Abraham's descendants from the rest of the world and serve as a permanent reminder of God's covenant with them.

Israel

Abraham and Sarah had a son just like God promised, and they named him Isaac. Isaac had a son named Jacob, and Jacob had twelve sons as well. Later in his life, Jacob would be renamed Israel, and his sons were instrumental in multiplying the descendants of Abraham into the full nation of Israel. The books of Exodus through Deuteronomy tell the story of how God used a man named Moses to save the Israelites from years of slavery in Egypt and bring them to the land of Canaan, which he had promised to Abraham years before. God continued to honor His covenant with Abraham and dwelt with the Israelites, but the Israelites continuously rebelled against God's leadership. They worshiped other gods and lived in sin, but God never gave up on them. God stayed true to His covenant and kept His promise to Abraham even when the Israelites disobeyed and rejected Him.

God is holy, so the only way He could dwell with the Israelites was for them to be holy as well. To accomplish this, God revealed His law to Moses so that Moses could write it down and teach it to the Israelites. The Law included instructions on cleanliness, the tabernacle, family matters, and various other issues. In Exodus 20, God gave the Israelites the Ten Commandments as a summary of the whole Law, and the books of Leviticus through Deuteronomy go into more detail about the Law. By keeping God's Law and serving Him, the Israelites would show the surrounding nations that their God was the true God. God's Law was a gift of grace to the world, demonstrating humanity's need for God and God's love and His desire to have a relationship with both the Israelites and the rest of the world.

One important aspect of the Law was sacrifice. When the Israelites disobeyed God's law, they repented and offered blood sacrifices of clean animals to cover their sins. Without the shedding of blood there could be no forgiveness of sins. However, the people continued to sin and the Israelites treated the sacrifices like insincere rituals instead of the necessary component to maintaining their relationship with God. Eventually, the people completely rejected God's rule and demanded a human king like the other nations around them. Rather than being a people set apart, they desired to become like the rest of the world.

Yet, God still used the Israelites' disobedience for the good of the world. He gave them a king just like they asked, and He promised that the Messiah would come through the line of one of their kings, King David. King David was also a descendant of Abraham, so God also stayed faithful to His covenant with Abraham. This Messiah would accomplish the salvation that the animal sacrifices could not. He would shed His blood as a single, permanent sacrifice that would pay the price for the sins of the whole world. This Messiah would be the one promised in Genesis 3 who would defeat death and sin forever.

Jesus

God provided the Law to the Israelites to demonstrate to them just how fallen and sinful they were. God knew that humanity could never live up to the perfect Law which He provided through Moses, and we proved Him correct through our consistent disobedience. The entire Old Testament is full of prophecies and promises of a coming Savior, and the Israelites waited and yearned for God to send this Messiah.

Then one, seemingly ordinary day, in the town of Nazareth, an angel appeared to a young virgin named Mary. This angel told Mary that she would give birth to the Son of God who would reign forever in the throne of God. She was to name this son Jesus, and He would save people from their sins. Jesus had been with God the Father from the very beginning, but He was about to come to earth and take on human form so that man could be reconciled and have their relationship with God restored. Jesus was God in the flesh. Mary gave birth to Jesus in the small town of Bethlehem, and she and her husband Joseph cared for Jesus as He grew and matured.

Jesus began His ministry when he was about thirty years old. He ate with the outcasts, healed the sick, and cast out demons. He revealed the hypocrisy of the religious leaders and accumulated crowds of thousands of people longing to hear His teaching concerning the Kingdom of God. He gathered twelve men in whom He invested personally, and these men became known as His twelve disciples. The gospels of Matthew, Mark, Luke, and John tell of Jesus' life and ministry during His time on earth, but as John writes, if every work of Jesus were recorded, "the world itself could not contain the books that would be written."

During His time on earth, Jesus did many good works and lived a completely perfect life, without sin. He is the only human who has ever lived without sin, and this is exactly why He was the perfect sacrifice that the rest of humanity needed. He was completely innocent, and yet one night, Judas, one of His twelve disciples, betrayed Him and handed Him over to be killed. Jesus knew this was coming, and He had warned His disciples that this would happen, but they still all fearfully abandoned Him when the soldiers came to take Him to His trial. Though He had committed no crime, Jesus endured torture, false accusations, and ultimately death by crucifixion. God the Father placed the sins of all humanity on Jesus while He was on the cross, and Jesus received the punishment that we all deserve.

But there's good news! Death was not the end for Jesus. After He died on the cross, Jesus was placed in a tomb sealed with a heavy stone. Three days later, two women went to Jesus' tomb to anoint His body with spices. However, when they arrived, they noticed that the stone was rolled away, and an angel declared that Jesus had resurrected from the dead! He had not only paid the punishment for our sins, but He had conquered death in the process. He revealed Himself to the two women, to His disciples, and appeared to many others after His resurrection.

Jesus ascended into heaven, and he now sits at the right hand of God, advocating for those who place their faith in Him.

Because He became human like us, He can sympathize with our temptations and weaknesses. He is interceding between us and the Father because He paid the price for our sins. Because of Jesus, we can know God personally, and when we place our faith in His death and resurrection rather than relying on our own efforts, we find salvation through our relationship with God.

Church

Those who have placed their faith in Christ are the church. Contrary to popular belief, the church is not a building but rather a group of people striving to serve God and make His name known to those around Him. Before He ascended into heaven, Jesus charged His disciples on earth to continue to spread His name across all nations and to develop more disciples of Him. He promised that He would always be with them and that His Holy Spirit would empower them to be His witnesses to the world.

The Holy Spirit descended onto the disciples on a day called Pentecost. You can read this account in Acts 2. The Holy Spirit grew the church's numbers by about three thousand on just that day alone! These disciples then went on to start the first church in a city called Antioch. The first church dedicated itself to listening to the disciples' teaching about God, fellowship with one another, and praying. They worked together to help those in need and to make the truth about Jesus known to their community. The Lord blessed them and grew their numbers daily.

It should be noted that the church is not perfect. The church is still made up of imperfect people who continue to sin. However, the difference is that the church is full of people striving to be like Christ and reflect Him to the world. God provided instruction for the church through His Word in the books of Acts through Revelation because He knows we are not perfect. And yet, despite our shortcomings, the Lord has continued to use His church to accomplish His mission of making disciples of all nations.

To this day, the church has continued to grow worldwide, and all followers of Jesus are part of one universal church. Jesus' command to make disciples of all nations applies to all people of the church. We do this by sharing what Christ has done for us and helping people grow in their faith through discipleship. As a college student, you can participate in this mission by sharing with your classmates and friends. It is also incredibly important for you to find your own local church family because they will encourage you and support you in your efforts. A local church family will also help you grow in your own relationship with God through discipleship and teaching. We are not designed to live without community, and the Lord has designed the church to fulfill this need.

Restoration

One day in the future, Jesus will return to earth and bring all things to their perfect resolution. The book of Revelation tells of Christ's second coming. When He returns, Christ will defeat sin and the devil once and for all, and all people on earth will worship Him and confess that He is Lord. He will judge all people, and those who have placed their faith in Him will be glorified. The Lord will create a new heaven and a new earth, and the church will reign forever alongside Him. All things will be made right, and God will bring about perfect justice to the world. People from all tribes, tongues, and nations will come together to sing His praises and enjoy God's presence forevermore.

Conclusion

This entire story of how God desires a relationship with humanity is called **the gospel.** You can find this entire narrative displayed throughout Scripture, but we are not only called to respond and receive salvation through the gospel. We are also called to share it with others because those who do not receive salvation through the gospel will be separated from God forever. The church will get to enjoy God's presence in eternity, and we want to bring as many people with us into that joy as possible. We are still in the age of the church, and the Holy Spirit is still working through believers to bring people from all nations to Himself. He wants to use you, but you have to make the choice to take action and follow His calling.

We want all people to have the chance to respond to God's offer of salvation, but they can only do that if you share the gospel with them. The entire narrative of the Bible is true and important, and if you study and learn it, you will be able to steer conversations and share this gospel with others. God loves all people and desires a relationship with Him, and this is all revealed through His Word. I'm going to leave you with one question: **Who will you share this gospel with today?**

Additional Resources

Biblical Theology by Nick Roark & Robert Cline
A Reader's Guide to the Bible by John Goldingay
The Old Testament by Richard Hess
The New Testament in Antiquity by Gary Burge, Lynn Cohick, and Gene Green
The Jesus Storybook Bible by Sally-Lloyd Jones (Yes it's a kids book but it's great so you should read it.)
The Baker Illustrated Bible Dictionary by Tremper Longman
Commentary sets that may be helpful: *Christ Centered Exposition, Wiersbe Exposition Commentary, Bible Speaks Today, New American Commentary, and The NIV Application Commentary.*
Ultimately, pick up your Bible and begin reading today!

TWO

༺৩৫৹

Relationships

"Love consists in this: not that we loved God, but
that He loved us and sent His son to be the atoning
sacrifice for our sins. Dear friends, if God loved us
in this way, we also must love one another."
1 John 4:10-11

The second letter of C.R.A.S.H. stands for "Relationships." Our
lives center around relationships. We have relationships with God,
with our families, with our friends, and even with strangers. From
the very beginning, God declared that it was not good for man to
be alone and created the first woman to be his companion (Gen.
2:18). Since we were created to live in relationship with others, it
is imperative that we choose those relationships carefully. Proverbs
13:20 states,

"The one who walks with the wise will become
wise, but a companion of fools will suffer harm."

Those we spend time with will influence us even when we don't realize it. For the Christian, it's even more important to surround ourselves with a team of encouragers who will spur you on as you share the gospel with others.

In this section, we're going to focus on two types of relationships that will affect not only your college experience, but the rest of your life. Your relationships with God and His church will determine everything you do because as a Christian these are your two main sources of growth. It's important that you establish these relationships now as a college student because even though it seems that you're in your busiest stage of life, it will only get more difficult as life progresses. Start valuing your time with God and serving in His church now, and if you don't know where to start, your BCM director or pastor would love to help you!

Relationship with God

The most important relationship you will ever have is your relationship with God. Yes, you read that right. The almighty God who created the universe wants to have a relationship with **YOU.** From the beginning, God created humanity so that He could dwell with them and know them, and He continues to desire that level of intimacy with us to this day. In fact, God sent His only Son to die and come back to life so that we can know Him and be with Him for eternity. How cool is that?!

However, a relationship with God is a two-way street. He loves you, but you also have to love Him. Because of Adam and Eve's sin in the beginning, each of us has a disposition to reject Him. When we push past this tendency and recognize how much we need Him, our relationship with God begins. Romans 10:9-10 tells us how we can enter into this relationship with God:

"If you confess with your mouth, 'Jesus is Lord,' and believe in your heart that God raised him from the dead, you will be saved. One believes with the heart, resulting in righteousness, and one confesses with the mouth, resulting in salvation."

All you have to do to begin your relationship with God is to recognize and confess that you are a sinner and believe that Jesus has paid the price for your salvation. Now that you've accepted Christ and received salvation, you should seek to continue to grow closer to God and know Him more. Here are four ways to help you grow in your relationship to God:

1. **Seek.** God is perfect, so our priority must be to seek Him and know Him rather than His blessings. God does bless us, but if we love Him only because of His blessings, we are missing the point. God is enough for us, and we will grow immensely in our relationship with Him when we realize this.

   But how do we seek God? Practically, this looks like reading His Word and praying. He reveals Himself and speaks to us through the Bible, and when we pray, we speak directly to Him. One of the most important habits you can establish in your life as a college student is a daily time spent with God. Take time every day, whether in the morning when you wake up, at night before you sleep, or in the middle of the day, to read the Bible and pray. God will speak to you and reveal Himself to you when you make intentional efforts to know Him.

2. **Trust.** God is always faithful, which makes Him completely trustworthy. We don't have to worry about anything because God has all things under His control. This does not mean that life will always be easy, but it does mean that He will be with us and guide us as we pursue His will.

   One practical way that you can improve your trust in God is by journaling. Throughout Scripture, God commands His people to build monuments and tell stories to remember what He did for them in the past so that they can better trust Him in the present. This concept is still relevant to us today. When you see the Lord's, faithfulness come through in your life, tell someone about it. Not only that but write it down in a journal so that when you doubt in the future (and I guarantee that you will), you can look back and remember that the Lord was faithful in the past and have confidence that He continues to be trustworthy now.

3. **Obey.** Because God is perfect and faithful, He is worthy of our obedience. God's Word is full of commands for His people, and we are responsible to obey His commands. Jesus said in Matthew 22:37-39 that all His commands can be summarized in this way: Love God with all of your heart, soul, and mind and love your neighbor as yourself.

   As a college student, you can obey God now. You don't have to wait until you're older to follow His commands. As you go about your daily life, you can share the gospel with your peers and show them kindness. Invite your friends to BCM or church events with you, ask them to study a book of the Bible with you, or even simply sit and chat with the person in the cafeteria who looks like they're alone. The bottom line is: the way that you live your life should point your classmates to the One who you live for.

4. **Worship.** Our ultimate goal in everything that we do should be to glorify God. Every person who we share the gospel with, every blessing we receive, and even every trial that comes our way is an opportunity for us to glorify God. We glorify God when we obey Him, and He is worthy of our obedience because He is all that we need and always faithful.

   As we seek God and get to know Him more, it should automatically evoke worship from us. We also worship

God by obeying and serving Him joyfully. When we share the gospel and disciple others, we are worshiping God. We also worship God through giving Him thanks for all He has done and giving Him the glory for every blessing that comes our way. Not only that, but we thank Him for how He is faithful to be present with us in the hard times as well.

Each step of the cycle feeds into the next. The more you seek God, the more you trust Him. The more you trust Him, the more willing you will be to obey His commandments. As you obey His commandments, you worship Him. As you worship Him, you gain more knowledge of Him and seek Him again. You will struggle along the way, but as long as you are pursuing this process, your relationship with God will flourish. As your relationship with God grows, so will your relationship to those around you, especially with other believers in the church.

Church

When you have a relationship with God, you become a part of the church. Many of you are familiar with the church, but you might have a variety of opinions concerning it. Some of you have grown up in the church and love it. However, some of you have unfortunately been hurt by the church. The church makes mistakes because it is full of imperfect people, but God chooses to use it to take His gospel to the world. In this section, we are going to look at what God designed the church to be and how we can all work together to help the church realize that purpose.

Theologian Wayne Grudem states, "Church is the community of all true believers for all time."[2] The church is both local and global. All Christians around the world make up the church. This means that the church is made up of born-again believers of many cultures, languages, and people. At the same time, the global church is divided into local congregations. Each local congregation is a part of the global church, but they are independent and function as their own system. This model of both a global and local church has existed from the beginning of the church that we read about in the book of Acts and in Paul's letters.

According to Jonathan Leeman in his book *Church Membership: How the World Knows Who Represents Jesus*, five key components make up the church:

1. **Group of Christians.** The church is made up of people who have trusted in Christ for their salvation. The individual groups make up the local church, but each local church is a part of the larger, global church.
2. **A Regular Gathering.** The individual congregations have regular, usually weekly, gatherings to worship and study Scripture. These include both small group and corporate worship gatherings.
3. **Congregational Accountability.** In the local church, the authority goes to the entire congregation in matters of discipline and doctrine. This means that the church chooses its leaders and members.
4. **Purpose is to Represent Christ on Earth.** The church's purpose is to represent Christ to those around them. Each member is expected to strive for holiness and to hold one another accountable when they see a fellow member living in sin. The church should also serve others by reaching their surrounding communities' needs and sharing the gospel.
5. **Use of Preaching and Ordinances.** During the regular gatherings, the Word of God is preached, whether by a pastor or another church leader. In addition, the ordinances of the Lord's Supper and Baptism are a part of the regular life of the church. The church takes the Lord's

Supper to remind us of Christ's death and resurrection, and we baptize those who are ready to make a public profession of faith.[3]

These components are specifically referencing a Baptist church model, so there is some variation within different denominations. This variation especially shows itself concerning congregational authority because some churches have a different structure. However, the other four components are universal across the board for what makes up a Biblical church.

Another important aspect of your relationship with the church is membership. By becoming a member of a church, you are committing to serve and contribute to the life of the church. Your church family will encourage you to pursue obedience and help you grow in your relationship with God. You will also gain lasting discipleship relationships with older believers that will last long after college. The BCM is great, but it is no replacement for the local church. When you graduate, the BCM will become a great memory, but the church will go with you no matter where the Lord takes you after college.

Now that you understand the importance of the local church, how do you find a place to serve in it? It is not enough to simply attend church. Showing up every Sunday to the worship service and becoming another face in the crowd won't give you fulfillment. Instead, get involved and find your place where you can use your God-given talents to better the church. Are you good with children? Volunteer in the nursery. Are you musically gifted? Help with the worship team. Do you have a passion for teenagers? Offer to lead a youth small group.

No matter where you fit, the church needs you. You have a gift that no one else does, and God desires to use you to further His kingdom. The church is more than a building, it is people. You are the church, so go out and be the church!

Romantic Relationships

We couldn't let a chapter on "relationships" pass without discussing one last important relationship you will encounter during your college years: Romantic Relationships. Your relationships with God and with the church should always take priority in your life, but God created romance and marriage. It will be a part of many of your lives, so we would be doing a disservice to you if we neglected a brief discussion on dating.

While God does call some to singleness and not everyone finds their future spouse in college, the reality is that you are in a stage of life during which dating is prominent in your mind. Inspired by his own dating experience in college, Quinton has put together a few tips to help you navigate your romantic relationships:

1. Work on becoming the right person instead of trying to find the right person. Your expectations should mirror who you are.
2. Date only a GROWING Christian. Only over time can you find out if they are growing, so don't rush anything.
3. Develop a strong friendship first. This does not happen over text for a week and hanging out a couple of times.
4. Take things slow in the relationship. You grow into love; you fall into lust.
5. Establish boundaries before you date. No sex before marriage. Guard each other emotionally, physically, and spiritually. If they disregard boundaries and keep pressuring you, get out.
6. Write down your non-negotiables of what you want from a person in the relationship. This may include: growing believer, character traits, personal choices like outdoors person, or if they have more than three teeth.

7. Must have a strong community and around you. Have friends hold you accountable that are close to you. Have a mentor couple within the church that will help you with the relationship to not make mistakes as well as just seeing a godly marriage.
8. Hang out with other friends, together and individually. Continue to make an effort fostering friendships together.
9. Have check-ups throughout the relationship. This will help you to evaluate the relationship moving forward and to see how God is growing each of you.
10. Understand everyone has baggage in some way. You need to work through as much baggage as you can individually before getting in a relationship and not be each other's counselors or confidants in a dating relationship.

These ten tips are designed to help you navigate your romantic relationships in a wise manner. God cares about how you date, and these guidelines are a starting point to help you honor him as you date, not only during your college years, but throughout the rest of your life as well. Marriage is not a guarantee for Christians, but for those who are called to marriage, it is important to honor God as you navigate romance. The world will tell you that dating will give you meaning, but God is the One who defines your purpose. Your romantic relationships are meant to drive you closer to God, not further away from Him. This is why you must always put your relationship with God first in your life. You must be content in Him before you can begin pursuing someone else.

Conclusion

Relationships are important. Everyone operates in relationship with others, whether in a positive or negative way. Our charge to you after reading this chapter is this: evaluate the relationships in your life and your expectations for them. Are there ways that you need to improve? Are there some relationships in your life that tear you away from your relationship with the Lord? Are you involved in church, and if you aren't, how can you begin to find a local church where you can get plugged in?

God created humans to live in relationships, and Christians are no exception. While each of us is called to individually share Christ's love with others, we are not to work alone. In our relationship with God, He will provide us with strength and guidance as we pursue His will for our lives. Our relationship with the church encourages us to grow more in our relationship with God, and the church is God's chosen vessel to share the gospel with the world. The two go hand-in-hand, and neither one can be neglected.

Haylee's Church Experience

Throughout college, I attended multiple churches. I never truly committed to one church because I felt that I was too busy to serve in church. I worked multiple ministry internships and held a leadership position in the Baptist Student Union (my campus ministry), so I made excuses like "I'm already involved in ministry in other places." Without realizing it, I treated the BSU as my church, and when I graduated I realized that I would not keep my BSU family forever. I was missing the true community that came from the local church.

My home church growing up has been a blessing to me throughout my life. Even when I was in college two hours away, they prayed for me and supported me. I may not have developed a church family in college, but my home church has shown me the benefits of involvement in a local church. When I visit, the church knows me and values me. They've set the bar high, and when I moved to a new state to attend seminary, I knew I wanted a church family like that of my home church.

In college, I learned why the local church is important, and I had a great example of a church to look for when I moved for seminary. This combination brought me to a great local church, and I'm actively serving and learning from my new church family. My hope is that you don't make the same mistake I made in college. I pray that you see from my experience that the local church is important and worth the investment. It's ok to take some time to try out multiple churches to find which one fits your personality and meets your needs, but make sure finding one church and sticking with it is one of your priorities.

Additional Resources:

Concerning your relationship with God:
Knowing God by J.I. Packer
Something Needs to Change by David Platt
Abide in Christ by Andrew Murray
The Power of Knowing God by Tony Evans

Concerning your relationship with the church:
The Trellis and the Vine by Colin Marshall and Tony Payne
The Church Today by Paul Powell
Sojourners and Stranger:The Doctrine of the Church by Gregg Allison

Concerning your dating relationships:
Single, Dating, Engaged, Married by Ben Stuart
The New Rules for Love, Sex, and Dating by Andy Stanley
Boundaries in Dating by Henry Cloud and John Townsend
Things I Wish I'd Known Before We Got Married by Gary Chapman
Getting Ready for Marriage by Jim Burns and Doug Fields
The Meaning of Marriage by Timothy Keller

THREE

Answers

"But in your hearts regard Christ the Lord as holy,
ready at any time to give a defense to anyone who
asks you for a reason for the hope that is in you."
1 Peter 3:15

The "A" in C.R.A.S.H. stands for "Answers." Your college years
are full of people looking for answers, whether they're looking for
the answers to test or homework questions, answers to what their
major should be, or answers to deeper issues like the purpose of
life. Many will try to give you the answers you're seeking, and
they will supply you with advice whether you request it or not.
Your classmates, family, professors, and even your church will tell
you what to do and what to believe, and as a student you will have
to learn who you should and should not listen to.

The purpose of this chapter is not to give you life advice,
but rather to help you understand what should be the foundation
of every decision that you make: **your faith**. Your faith should
dictate every other facet of your life, but your faith is also the

aspect of your life which is most susceptible to questioning from others. Hebrews 11:1 states,

"Now faith is the reality of what is hoped for, the proof of what is not seen."

This verse defines faith, and one of the key characteristics of faith is that it is belief in something or someone that you cannot see. Because we cannot physically see God with our own eyes—although some such as Moses have seen Him—we require faith to believe in Him.

You will encounter many people who will challenge your beliefs and tell you that your faith is incorrect. When this happens, you must be ready to defend your faith, but you cannot do this effectively unless you critically evaluate what you believe. Because we are humans, we will never be able to fully comprehend God or answer every question concerning Him, but that does not mean we sit idly by and never study arguments for His existence. The act of defending your faith and proving the truth of Christianity is called **Apologetics**, and this chapter seeks to teach you some basic apologetic methods. You will gain some tools that will help you examine your own faith and answer some of the most common questions that you will encounter from others. This chapter will be divided into three sections: Suffering, Salvation, and Story.

The suffering section will strive to answer one of the most popular questions that Christians receive in regard to their beliefs–the question of suffering and evil in the world. This will lead us into the Salvation section, where we will discuss the reason why Christ came to earth to die and resurrect from the dead. In chapter two, we discussed how someone can have a relationship with God through faith in Christ, but it is also important that you know why He had to come to earth in the first place. Last but not least, the third section of this chapter, Story, will stress the importance of your own testimony when it comes to witnessing to those around you. If God has changed your life, you have a story to tell others, and we will talk about some methods for sharing your story.

Suffering

"If there is a good God out there, why is there so much evil and suffering in the world?" This is one of the most puzzling questions for non-believers and believers alike. You yourself have probably asked this question, but even if you haven't, it is one that you will face at some point in your life. Poverty, injustice, and disaster run rampant in our world, and Christians cannot ignore the obvious existence of these things. However, we can offer hope in the midst of it and provide answers to those who are seeking the good in the midst of the evil, and that is precisely what God calls to do. In this section on Suffering, we will discuss where evil originated from and why God allows it to continue.

Where Did Sin Originate?

At the center of every discussion concerning God and suffering is this question: Did God create sin? To find the answer to this question, we have to look back at Genesis chapters 1 through 3—the Creation and Fall of man. In Genesis chapter 1, a phrase repeats itself every time God creates something new: "and God saw that it was good." This means that God created all things to be perfect and pure, lacking sin. God could not create anything that does not line up with His character, and He is holy. Therefore, He could only create that which was holy. Sin is the opposite of what is holy because sin is disobedience and rebellion against God. If God could not create anything that is not good and holy, then he could not have created sin. However, if God did not create sin, we still must answer the question of how it came into the world. Unfortunately, this is where our part as humans comes into play. In chapter one, you read the whole narrative of Christianity from Creation to Restoration. The second part of that story is called "The Fall" which tells the story of man's disobedience and rebellion against God and how sin entered the world as a result. Adam and Eve did not believe that God knew what was best for them, and the serpent convinced them that God was deliberately keeping knowledge from them. The truth is that God was, in fact, keeping Adam and Eve from the knowledge of good and evil, but it was for their good. They had perfect communion with God, but once they chose to disobey God, they lost that relationship, which led to their death.

Therefore, sin came into the world because humanity chose it over their relationship with God. In his namesake book, James writes about the cause of sin and God's role in how sin affects the world. In chapter 1 verses 13 through 15, he writes,

> "No one undergoing a trial should say, "I am being tempted by God," since God is not tempted by evil, and he himself doesn't tempt anyone. But each person is tempted when he is drawn away and enticed by his own evil desire. Then after desire has conceived, it gives birth to sin, and when sin is fully grown, it gives birth to death."

This verse tells us that God does not cause sin or suffering. These things are a part of human nature because Adam and Eve sinned in the beginning. In Romans chapter 5, the Apostle Paul clearly describes this concept, telling us that sin came into the world through the disobedience of one man (Adam), but he doesn't stop there. Paul also writes that the death of one man, Jesus Christ, brought justification for humanity. In verse 18 he summarizes this idea, stating,

"So then, as through one trespass there is condemnation for everyone, so also through one righteous act there is justification leading to life for everyone."

The only person to live on this earth without sin was Jesus Christ, and He achieved that because He was equally God and man. Because of His sacrifice on the cross, all people can experience reconciliation and restoration. However, while this is wonderful news, we still have to deal with the problem of sin and suffering while we are here on earth. We've seen that God Himself does not cause sin, but the question remains, "Why does he allow sin and suffering to continue?" You will often be confronted with this question, so it is important that you understand how to answer it. There is a certain degree to which we cannot fully know God's ways, but He does reveal much through His Word. In the following section we will learn some reasons why God continues to allow sin and suffering to afflict this world.

Why Does God Allow Sin and Suffering to Continue to His Followers?

When you first became a believer, did you think that all of your problems would just disappear? That you would never experience another hardship again? Many people have this idea, and while faith in Jesus does bring unexplainable joy, it does not eliminate suffering from our lives. In fact, Jesus told the apostles in Matthew 10:16-18,

"Look, I'm sending you out like sheep among wolves. Therefore, be as shrewd as serpents and as innocent as doves. Beware of them, because they will hand you over to local courts and flog you in their synagogues. You will even be brought before governors and kings because of me, to bear witness to them and to the Gentiles."

Jesus tells them that persecution is a guarantee. This is not the most pleasing thing to hear, but it is important for all Christians to understand. The life that Jesus calls us to is not an easy one, and while as Christians in the United States we are not often being flogged and arrested for our faith, on the college campus you will be ridiculed by your peers and even some of your professors because you are a follower of Jesus.

Many people will not understand why you continue to follow Jesus when things get hard, but Jesus gives comfort later in that same chapter of Matthew. He tells the disciples that The Father knows them and loves them, and though they will struggle and possibly die for their faith, God sees them and honors their commitment to Him. We can take heart that our suffering has purpose. God does not cause sin and suffering in the world, but He does use it for our ultimate good.

Peter tells us why God allows His followers to experience trials and suffering in 1 Peter 1:6-7. He writes,

> "You rejoice in this, even though now for a short time, if necessary, you suffer grief in various trials so that the proven character of your faith --- more valuable than gold which, though perishable, is refined by fire --- may result in praise, glory, and honor at the revelation of Jesus Christ."

God allows His followers to struggle because it improves their reliance upon Him. He uses suffering to test our faith, and the purpose of this testing is to ultimately bring Him glory. When non-Christians watch us rejoice in our trials and glorify God through them, they notice. One of the stories that most often comes to mind when I think about suffering is the life of Joseph in Genesis chapters 37 through 50. Joseph's brothers sold him into slavery, and Potiphar falsely imprisoned him, but in the end, he recognizes that what his enemies meant for evil, God used for good. Because Joseph was in Egypt, he was able to provide for his family during a famine. God was in control the whole time, but Joseph had to go through hardship to accomplish God's ultimate good. Joseph's faith was tested, but ultimately, he gave God all the glory, which is exactly what Peter says is supposed to happen.

But what about those who haven't placed their faith in Christ? Why does the Lord allow them to suffer as well? The answer to that goes back to our discussion on sin. Because humanity is fallen and separated from God, those who do not have hope in Jesus will face hardships just like Christians will. The difference is non-Christians have no hope. They do not see the purpose in their trials.

However, God does use suffering to bring non-Christians to Himself just as he uses it to strengthen the faith of Christians. He may be trying to get their attention, as He did with Saul in Acts chapter 9. When people have no hope and nowhere else to turn, God uses those circumstances to show them His love and to reveal Himself as a light in the darkness.

When you are on your campus or walking around your community, and you notice someone who might be suffering, take a minute and talk to them. You might find that God placed you there so that you could show them how to have hope in the midst of their struggle. Not only can they have hope, but they can have confidence that in the end God will bring about justice and work things out for good and for His glory. You can explain how they can have a relationship with God, and the next section which speaks on "Salvation" will equip you to have those precise conversations.

The Suffering of Jesus Christ (a note from Haylee)

> "For we do not have a high priest who is unable to sympathize with our weaknesses, but one who has been tempted in every way as we are, yet without sin. Therefore, let us approach the throne of grace with boldness, so that we may receive mercy and find grace to help us in time of need." - Hebrews 4:15-16

Did you know that Jesus Himself experienced hard times? He experienced every facet of humanity, including trials and temptations. He was tempted by Satan, kicked out of His hometown, abandoned by His closest friends, and even put to death because of false accusations. He didn't come into the world and live a perfect life because it was easy. He came and lived a perfect life while also going through the same things that we do today.

Why is this important? If we have a Savior who can sympathize with our struggles, we can approach Him in confidence knowing that He understands what we are going through. He's been there, done that, and He knows how to get us through even the toughest of times.

What a great comfort that is! Knowing that no matter what hardships I face, my Savior knows how I feel and what I'm experiencing. He isn't distant, but He is right in the thick of it all with me, extending grace and mercy to me in the middle of the storm.

Salvation

As you have conversations with people on your college campuses and in your communities, you will meet many who will try to convince you that Christianity is "too restrictive" or "too harsh" because of the claim that no one can come to faith except through Jesus. However, it is important to note that in reality, Christianity is the only faith which boasts of a Savior who came into this world to save us. Every other faith, whether it be Islam, Hinduism, Animism, etc. is all about humanity being "good enough" to reach God or enlightenment, but Christianity tells of a Savior who came to earth to pay the penalty for our sins because God knows that on our own, we cannot reach Him. It is the only religion with a true concept of grace. When you meet people of other religions, this fact is what you should highlight. Show them how Christianity does not rely on human achievement and that through Jesus we can know for certain that we have been made right with God as opposed to aimlessly hoping we do enough good things in this life to get us into heaven.

In addition to those who follow other religions, you will encounter many people who do not believe in God at all–atheists. Atheists do not believe that anything exists outside of the material world, meaning there is no need for salvation because there is nothing we need to be saved from. They live without divine purpose because they have nothing to strive for besides human achievements. For atheists, an effective conversation starter is simply asking them what they believe to be their purpose. Often, they will respond with something along the lines of making enough money, finding success in a career, or maybe even doing enough good deeds in this world so that they can leave a positive legacy after they die. As a Christian, you can offer them hope of something even greater. You can demonstrate to them that your purpose is not dependent on this world and that you have hope in Someone who offers so much more than success in this temporary world.

While not everyone that you meet will fit into these two categories, many will. If you are not able to defend your salvation and explain why Jesus Christ is the only way to restore our relationship with God, you will miss opportunities to show those whom you meet what true hope looks like. We have already discussed in chapter two how you can find salvation, but because it is so vital to how you witness to others, we are going to study it again. If you are going to defend your faith, you must understand how and why Christ came to earth to give salvation to all people. Let's start with a definition.

> Salvation is the work of God, through the death and resurrection of His son Jesus Christ, to deliver all who believe in Him from sin so that they can find restoration and experience a relationship with Him once again.

God desires to bestow salvation upon all people, though many will reject Him and choose to worship other gods or to pursue their own sinful desires. This choice will lead them into separation from God for eternity, and they will face judgment for their sin and lack of repentance. On the other hand, those who repent from their sinful ways and place their faith in the sacrifice and resurrection of Jesus Christ will find salvation. It is important that you recognize that Jesus Christ is the **only** means of salvation because many will try to convince you otherwise. No amount of good works can save you, and no other religion or faith offers salvation either.

Through the life, death, and resurrection of Jesus our salvation was completely paid for, we must also repent and put our faith wholly in Jesus in order to be in right relationship with God. This involves faith and repentance. In order to believe in Christ, we must have faith that the Bible is true, and that Christ's death and resurrection is enough for our salvation. There is nothing any person can do to achieve salvation on our own. We must rely on Christ, and this can be intimidating. However, as we put our faith in Christ, we also must turn from our own sinful ways and acknowledge our own weaknesses. This process is called repentance.

Repentance means agreeing with God that we are sinners in need of salvation, turning from our sinful desires, and making the conscious decision to strive to live like Christ. Of course, no one on earth will ever reach the perfect standard of Jesus, but when we repent, we acknowledge that we are trying. We are no longer satisfied with living in sin, and we strive for God's holy standard. The world will not understand this because they are still living in sin, but your job is to show them through your actions and words that a life in sin is nothing compared to a life of following Christ. And that is what this C.R.A.S.H. Course is designed to help you with.

To help you better understand the process of salvation, here are some terms that are helpful to know. We encourage you to become familiar with these terms so that you can engage in conversation with others as well as expand your theological knowledge as well. We have also included some verses alongside the definitions of each word so that you can better understand each term:

1. **Justification:** The moment when someone puts their faith in Christ and the work of Jesus is applied to them. therefore, their sins are forgiven and they are declared Righteous (2 Corinthians 5:21, Romans 5:1)
2. **Sanctification:** Once someone accepts Christ, the ongoing process of becoming holy like Christ. (1 Thessalonians 5:23, Romans 12:1, Ephesians 4:20-24)
3. **Glorification:** The future state of all believers in which they become perfect in Christ. (Colossians 3:4, 1 John 3:2, Romans 8:18-30)

Now that you have some of the vocabulary in your toolbox, it is important for you to know some Scripture to help you share the gospel with others. The following list of verses will assist you in explaining to people how they can find salvation and why it is necessary. You should become familiar with these verses so you can use them in your own gospel witness:

God desires all to come to salvation:
"This is good, and it pleases God our Savior, who wants everyone to be saved and to come to the knowledge of the truth." 1 Timothy 2:3-4

"He himself is the atoning sacrifice for our sins, and not only for ours, but also for those of the whole world." 1 John 2:2

Jesus is the only way to salvation:
"For God loved the world in this way: He gave his one and only Son, so that everyone who believes in him will not perish but have eternal life. For God did not send his Son into the world to condemn the world, but to save the world through him. Anyone who believes in him is not condemned, but anyone who does not believe is already condemned, because he has not believed in the name of the one and only Son of God." John 3:16-18

"For while we were still helpless, at the right time, Christ died for the ungodly. For rarely will someone die for a just person --- though for a good person perhaps someone might even dare to die. But God proves his own love for us in that while we were still sinners, Christ died for us. How much more then, since we have now been declared righteous by his blood, will we be saved through him from wrath. For if, while we were enemies, we were reconciled to God through the death of his Son, then how much more, having been reconciled, will we be saved by his life. And not only that, but we also rejoice in God through our Lord Jesus Christ, through whom we have now received this reconciliation." Romans 5:6-11

The Holy Spirit Seals our Salvation

"In him you also were sealed with the promised Holy Spirit when you heard the word of truth, the gospel of your salvation, and when you believed. The Holy Spirit is the down payment of our inheritance, until the redemption of the possession, to the praise of his glory." Ephesians 1:13-14

"He has also put his seal on us and given us the Spirit in our hearts as a down payment." 2 Corinthians 1:22

I encourage you to memorize these verses, as well as others that you find throughout Scripture, so that when someone asks you about your faith you can point them to the Bible. This will show them that you take your salvation seriously, and it will give them references that they can look back to later on their own time.

Story

The previous two sections of this chapter, suffering and salvation, have addressed issues that might arise in debates or discussions. We have given you various Scripture references and other tools to help you answer these questions, and we encourage you to continue your own studying in pursuit of greater understanding. We have included a list of resources at the end of this chapter to assist you in furthering your own apologetic research. This section, however, will address something that you know very well and that no one can dispute: your story.

One of the most effective forms of sharing the gospel is simply sharing your testimony. Your testimony is your story for how you came to know Christ and how he has changed your life. This section will focus on how to streamline your story so that you can share it quickly and effectively. Your story is important because no one can question it. Unlike when you're sharing facts or arguing for something, no one can question your personal experience and say you are wrong. Not only that, but as a college student you can share your story throughout your day as you engage in conversation with your classmates and peers. It's an easy, non-confrontational witnessing tool.

But how do you even start the conversation? How do you get from small talk in the hallway to sharing your testimony? You have to be intentional with your conversations. Maybe you could invite the person to get lunch or coffee with you. Once you get into that slightly more intimate setting, you can turn the conversation to your testimony by asking, "do you mind if I share about Someone that has changed my life?" Or you can ask them to start by saying, "I would love to know more about you. Would you mind sharing your story with me?"

Both of these questions serve as a segue into a gospel presentation. Nowadays, people are used to shallow conversation because everyone is always rushed and distracted. However, when you show actual desire to go deeper and truly get to know someone, while they might be resistant at first, in the long run it will be a conversation that they will remember.

At the same time, because people do have short attention spans, it is important to learn how to share your testimony in a

short, 5-to-7-minute time span. You can share more details as you
get to know the person more, but to start out you want to keep it
simple and impactful. CRU, a campus ministry formerly known
as Campus Crusade for Christ, gives three steps to sharing your
story in 5 minutes:

1. **Before Following Christ** - In this section, you highlight
   how you lived before you knew Christ. This isn't about
   bragging about your past sins, but rather looking at how
   far you've come.
2. **How You came to Christ** - This is when you talk about
   that moment that you gave your life to Christ. In this
   section, you should specifically lay out the gospel. Don't
   just say how Christ came into your life but why you've
   chosen to trust him
3. **Your Life after Coming to Christ** - Answer the
   question, "how has knowing Christ changed the way
   that you live?" Be specific. Point out that you still fail
   sometimes because you aren't perfect, but highlight
   the Lord's forgiveness and how you now react to sin as
   opposed to before you knew Christ. [4]

As you can see, sharing your testimony isn't difficult. It does
require some practice though. Perhaps you could get together
with your friends and rehearse sharing your testimonies, timing
one another to ensure that you aren't too brief or going too long.
You can also come up with some follow up questions after you
share. Some questions you might ask are, "What did you think
about my story?" "Do you have any questions about Jesus or how
to have a relationship with Him? Or you could just get straight
to it and ask, "Would you like to also have a relationship with
Jesus Christ?"

When you share your story with others, God will move.
You might not see that person come to know Christ, but God

will honor your obedience. But the most important thing is that you share the truth of the gospel along with your testimony. The point is to make God, not ourselves, known, and He works in our lives so that we can tell others what he has done for us. That is ultimately what sharing your testimony is. It's talking about how God has moved in your life and demonstrating why He is worth following.

Haylee's Story

I grew up as a minister's kid, so I don't remember a time in my life when I didn't know the name of Jesus. When the doors of the church were open, I was there. I was incredibly fortunate to grow up in an environment where my parents told me about Jesus every day. However, I did live in darkness until I was 8 years old and started my relationship with Jesus. Even though I don't remember it well, I do know that I was living a sinful life just by the fact that I didn't have a relationship with Christ.

When I was 8, I prayed to accept Christ in my bedroom. After all of the Sunday School Lessons and time in church, I understood that I was a sinner and needed forgiveness. As an 8-year-old I was obviously not theologically savvy, but I knew that I did bad things and wanted to be God's friend. I had learned that I could be right with God by praying and accepting Him "into my heart," so that is exactly what I did. I was baptized a few months later by my dad.

Though my relationship with Christ has not been perfect, and I have failed many times, He has been faithful to sustain me and forgive me every time I mess up. As I read His Word and study it, I learn more about His character and grow to love Him more. He has guided me as I strive to follow His plan for my life, and I look forward to an eternity of knowing Him

Quinton's Story

Growing up, my family situation was a bit confusing. My mom had me when she was in high school and to this day, I have not met my father or even know who he is. My grandparents were the ones who raised me with my mom still around. My mom then brought home my brother when I was almost four; afterwards she got married and a year later was divorced. In the midst of witnessing that craziness, my grandparents were so loving and also loved the Lord. They brought me to church and taught me about who Jesus is. At five years old, I remember being at a church retreat and the pastor was sharing how Jesus died on the cross for my sins and how we need to have faith in the gospel of Jesus to have a right relationship with God who is our Father.

After placing my faith in Jesus, I began to follow Him by sharing my faith, knowing God's Word, and being in community with other believers. I was in a Christian school at the time and went to church two to three times a week so that was all I knew until we moved. This all changed when we moved to Florida and I enrolled in a public school where I quickly realized not everyone had heard of Jesus. Over time, I began to listen to my peers and what the world told me to do instead of looking to scripture. In high school, I made a lot of decisions that I am not proud of that eventually led to me getting arrested my junior year. After that I had to really think of the trajectory my life was taking so I sought wisdom from my youth pastor and the Bible. I realized I had grown selfish and prideful in high school and God, being a holy and loving Father, brought me back to Him through this arrest.

Once I went to college, I joined the Baptist Collegiate Ministries there. I began serving, teaching, and being mentored during that time and that really helped bring me where the Lord has me today.

Conclusion

We've really hammered on a lot of things in this chapter, and I hope each section has helped you because you will face all of these things—Suffering, Salvation, and Story—not only throughout college but in your everyday life as well. While this chapter did contain a lot of information, the goal is for you to have more answers for witnessing to others when they ask you difficult questions. They will ask you about why suffering is a part of the human experience. They will question your beliefs, and you must be ready to explain why your salvation in Jesus Christ is the only way to be reconciled to God. And as you share about your salvation, tell your testimony and talk about all the Lord has done in your life because that is one of your most powerful tools in your witnessing tool belt.

It is also our hope that now you have an even greater understanding of your faith and why you believe what you do. If you're not confident, it will be easier for people to discourage you and cause you to doubt. But when you have a strong foundation through studying God's Word and knowing Him better through prayer, you will be better equipped to follow the mandate from 1 Peter 3:15—to be prepared to give a defense for your hope.

Additional Resources

Visual Theology by Tim Challies and Josh Byers
Christian Theology by Millard Erickson
Reformed Dogmatics by Herman Bavinck
The New Evidence that Demands a Verdict by Josh McDowell
The Cross of Christ by John Stott
Making Sense of God by Timothy Keller
The Reason for God by Timothy Keller
Evil and the Justice of God by N. T. Wright

FOUR

ᘓᕙᖆᘖ

Servant

"If anyone serves me, he must follow me. Where
I am, there my servant also will be. If anyone
serves me, the Father will honor him."
John 12:26

The "S" in the CRASH acronym stands for "servant." As
Christians, we are called to be servants to the world around us, but
this is a completely different concept from what the western–or
more specifically, American–culture tells us. In her book, *Spiritual
Disciplines Handbook,* Adele Calhoun writes,

> "Many Americans spend their lives working
> themselves into a place where they can be served
> more than serve. Our culture sees the blessed ones
> as those who get waited on and served. And few
> among us aspire to be the maid with the job of
> serving and blessing others."[5]

The American culture has worked so hard to convince people that the goal in life is to have others work for you, to serve you. You go to college so you can get a good job that will one day make you the boss of others, and we look down on those who work what we consider "lower-level jobs" because they aren't in charge of anyone. The entire goal of a career is to "climb the ladder" and get more successful, and while this isn't inherently bad, Jesus calls us to live radically opposite from the rest of the world by being servants. In this chapter we will discuss four aspects of servanthood: the Christian call to servanthood, Jesus as the Perfect Servant, the traits of servanthood, and how to practically implement service into our everyday lives.

The Christian Call to Servanthood

All Christians have a call to servanthood, and this call is two-fold. We are called to serve Christ and to serve others. These feed into one another because as we serve Christ, we are inherently inclined to serve those around us as well. In fact, our greatest way of serving Christ is that we share the gospel with the people around us and pointing someone to the saving grace of Jesus Christ is the ultimate act of love we can do for someone.

But before we can get into the practicality of how we are to serve Christ, we must take a few minutes to contemplate the "why." Why do we serve Christ? The basic answer to this question is that we serve Christ because He came to earth as a servant to bring salvation to the world. We will look more closely at how Jesus exemplifies the Perfect Servant in the third section of this chapter, but let's briefly look at Mark 10:42-45 and Philippians 2:3-8 because both passages reveal Jesus' attitude of servanthood. Mark chapter 10 states:

"Jesus called them over and said to them, "You know that those who are regarded as rulers of the Gentiles lord it over them, and those in high positions act as tyrants over them. But it is not so among you. On the contrary, whoever wants to become great among you will be your servant, and whoever wants to be first among you will be a slave to all. For even the Son of Man did not come to be served, but to serve, and to give his life as a ransom for many.""

In this passage, Jesus is speaking to James and John after they requested to sit at His right and left hands in glory, meaning that they wanted to be lifted up and recognized for their devotion to Christ. They wanted credit. However, Jesus reveals that there should be no hierarchy among His followers because no one is greater than another. He takes it a step further to say that the real attitude of His followers must be that of servants because Jesus Himself came to serve and give His life. In Philippians, Paul reflects this same reasoning. He writes,

"Do nothing out of selfish ambition or conceit, but in humility consider others as more important than yourselves. Everyone should look out not only for his own interests, but also for the interest of others. Adopt the same attitude as that of Christ Jesus, who, existing in the form of God, did not consider equality with God as something to be exploited. Instead, he emptied himself by assuming the form of a servant, taking on the likeness of humanity. And when he had come as a man, he humbled himself by becoming obedient to the point of death --- even to death on a cross."

In Mark, Jesus tells the disciples that they are to serve others because that is exactly what He Himself came to do, and Paul reiterates this point in his letter to the Philippians. Paul encourages them to look out for others' interests because Jesus took on the form of a servant and died to bring salvation to the world. Because our Savior took on the form of a servant, we should as well.

Therefore, to answer the question, "why do we serve Christ?" is, quite simply, because Christ came to serve us, and He continues to do so as our advocate before the Father. 1 John 2 describes this well. He loved us enough to come down to our level and perform the ultimate act of service: dying on the cross to pay the penalty for our sins, and in return we should devote our lives to serving Him out of awe and gratitude.

The primary way in which we serve Christ is by serving those around us. This can take many forms, and we will discuss ways to practically serve in the final section of this chapter, but first we must recognize that our goal in serving others is not so that we ourselves can get recognition. We serve Christ because He served us first, but also so that God will ultimately get all the glory. Jesus teaches in Matthew 5:14-16:

> "You are the light of the world. A city situated on a hill cannot be hidden. No one lights a lamp and puts it under a basket, but rather on a lampstand, and it gives light for all who are in the house. In the same way, let your light shine before others, so that they may see your good works and give glory to your Father in heaven."

In these verses which occur in the middle of Jesus' Sermon on the Mount, Jesus teaches that his followers are to be light to the world around them, showing others the joy that salvation brings to our lives. However, He does not say that we are to be light so that others know who we are, but rather so that the Father will get the glory. Even non-believers are capable of serving others and showing kindness, but Christians have a different purpose in our service. Our goal is to share the gospel as we serve because we have a higher purpose, and that is what sets our form of service apart from that of the rest of the world.

Jesus as the Perfect Servant

Now that we've discussed why Christians are called to be servants, we can get into the practical traits of what a servant should look like. Servants of Christ are to be set apart from the world and to reflect the One whom they serve. They do this by studying the person of Christ and how He exemplified servanthood in His own ministry while on earth. In this section, we will look specifically at John 13 verses 12-15, the story of Jesus washing the disciples' feet:

> "When Jesus had washed their feet and put on his outer clothing, he reclined again and said to them, "Do you know what I have done for you? You call me Teacher and Lord --- and you are speaking rightly, since that is what I am. So, if I, your Lord and Teacher, have washed your feet, you also ought to wash one another's feet. For I have given you an example, that you also should do just as I have done for you."

During Jesus' last week before his crucifixion, Jesus takes some time to teach the disciples a special lesson, a lesson in servanthood. While the group was in the middle of eating supper, Jesus began to wash the disciples' feet, a chore which would have been reserved for the servants of the house. Jesus even washed the feet of Judas, who He knew would betray Him later that same week. By doing this, Jesus provided an example to his disciples, showing them that even the Son of God was willing to stoop down to such a humble level.

In verse 8 of chapter 13, Peter objects to Jesus washing his feet, protesting because He could not understand why their Savior would condescend to such a lowly level. However, Jesus corrects Peter and tells the disciples that the way He was serving them was the way in which they are to serve others. Jesus challenges them to put away pride and rethink their self-image. He called them to be leaders, but in order for them to truly lead they had to first learn to serve.

Jesus' example to the disciples is the same one which Christians today should follow. While our context does not involve us washing peoples' feet, it could mean handing out food to the homeless people we see on the streets or sitting with the student eating lunch by themselves in the cafeteria. What Jesus means when He tells us to follow His example of servanthood is that we must look out for chances to help people even when it is inconvenient or unpleasant for us. When we go out of our way to show people that we love them through service, we have more opportunities to share the gospel with people.

Traits of a Servant

While Jesus is the perfect example of a servant, Scripture also teaches us about other traits of servanthood, all of which Jesus emulates as well. In this section, we will explain four specific characteristics of a servant: humble, intentional, compassionate, and flexible. We will learn what the Bible says about these traits and how Christians are to use them as Christ did in His own ministry.

The first trait of a servant is **humility.** Humility is not simply looking down on yourself, but rather to think of yourself less. In his book, *Humility: The Journey Towards Holiness,* Andrew Murray writes, "Humility, once you think you have it, you've lost it... It is entire dependence on God. In light of God, we have seen ourselves to be nothing."[6] As humans, we have absolutely no right to be prideful about anything because God is greater and holier than us. He is the one who has the authority to be prideful, and He chooses humility instead. Paul expertly describes Christ's humility in Philippians 2:4-8, which you can read under "The Christian Call to Servanthood" heading for this chapter.

Jesus humbled Himself so much that He came to earth to die for the sins of all people. He did not have to do this; He could have left us in the mess of sin that we made for ourselves. And yet, just as He demonstrated when He washed the disciples' feet in John 13, Jesus cares for us and desires to serve us. This truth does not give us reason to boast, however. It compels us to do just as Jesus did and humble ourselves so that we can serve others and point them to the Gospel.

The second trait of a servant is **intentionality.** Intentionality means serving with purpose. As we go about our service, we are to intentionally use every opportunity possible to share the gospel with those we serve because ultimately that is what it is all about. In our humility, we are to give all glory to God for every gospel conversation and trust Him to use our faithfulness to grow His kingdom. It isn't about us. Paul writes in Ephesians 2:10:

> "For we are his workmanship, created in Christ
> Jesus for good works, which God prepared ahead
> of time for us to do."

God has already provided us with opportunities for service and good works, but it is our job to look out for them and take advantage of them.

Intentionality also plays into our attitudes when we serve others. We should not be reluctant and lazy, but rather we must be always eager and willing to do our best to help people. We must remember that we represent Christ, so when we roll our eyes or sigh as we help someone, what sort of image does that give them of Him? Our demeanors are just as important as the work we do. When Jesus washed the disciples' feet, He did so eagerly and in love, and as His servants, we are to do our work with the same attitude.

The third trait of a servant is **compassion**. A compassionate servant is one who serves even when there is no benefit for them. Even if no one ever knows that you helped that person, you still do it simply because you love them. Obviously, Jesus is the perfect example of a compassionate servant. He had nothing to gain by sacrificing Himself for the sins of humanity, but He did so anyway because of His love for us. The gospels are full of instances which describe Jesus' compassion:

> "When he saw the crowds, he felt compassion for them, because they were distressed dejected, like sheep without a shepherd." - Matthew 9:36

> "I have compassion on the crowd, because they've already stayed with me three days and have nothing to eat." - Mark 8:2

> "When the Lord saw her, he had compassion on her and said, "Don't weep." - Luke 7:13

These verses are only a few of the many throughout the gospels that describe Jesus' compassion towards those who followed after Him. He healed and fed people, meeting their physical needs, but He also longed to meet their spiritual needs as well.

In the same way, we, as followers of Christ, are to have compassion for the needy around us. We are to seek opportunities to meet their physical needs and point them to Jesus so that He can meet their spiritual needs as well. Our compassion is what will set us apart from the rest of the world because we do not desire to take credit for our service. We point back to the reason why we serve–because Jesus calls us to love everyone just as He does with no exceptions.

Last but certainly not least, the fourth trait of a servant is **flexibility.** When things go awry and don't happen the way we want, instead of getting mad and giving up, we take a deep breath and follow the Holy Spirit's guidance. Sometimes the Holy Spirit shakes up our plans because He has another purpose for us, and I can guarantee that what He has for you is much better than what you could have imagined for yourself. Paul writes in Galatians 5:25,

> "If we live by the Spirit, let us also keep in step with the Spirit."

This verse emphasizes the importance of staying in tune with the Holy Spirit's guidance. As followers of Christ, we must rely on the Holy Spirit to lead us and show us opportunities for service that might be different from what we originally intended.

One example in which flexibility is required is a mission trip. Traveling will always require people to get out of their comfort zone, and almost always something goes wrong. However, sometimes when the plan changes, that is actually the Spirit wrecking our own expectations so that we can serve those He actually intends for us to meet. One example of this in the Bible is Paul and the Macedonian Call in Acts 16:6-10. Paul traveled throughout the region of Phrygia and Galatia, trusting the Holy Spirit to show Him where to go. One night, Paul had a vision of a Macedonian man urging him to come, and Paul did exactly that. Macedonia was not in Paul's original plans, but he was flexible and harkened to the Spirit.

Humility, Intentionality, Compassion, and Flexibility are four traits that a servant must embrace in order to be effective. We look to Jesus and the Bible to show us how to implement these traits into our lives, and we trust the Holy Spirit to use us to serve others when we live like Christ. However, just as there are traits of a servant, there are also traits which are enemies of servanthood. These qualities make service more difficult and hinder our gospel witness, and they are **slothfulness** and **pride**.

Slothfulness is the first enemy of servitude. Slothfulness is, simply, laziness. In the book of wisdom, Proverbs, Solomon writes many times against the slothful person. In chapter 13 verse 4 he writes,

> "The slacker craves, yet has nothing, but the diligent is fully satisfied."

While this verse is not specifically referencing service, the principle remains the same. The Lord values diligence, and laziness is not acceptable. Paul echoes God's disapproval of slothfulness in Romans 12:11, 13,

> "Do not lack diligence in zeal; be fervent in the Spirit, serve the Lord. Share with the saints in their needs; pursue hospitality."

Paul tells us that we are to serve the Lord with zeal and meet the needs of others. We are to work as unto the Lord in all that we do, and that includes our service. However, sometimes when we are working diligently and serving the Lord, we can face the second enemy of servitude: Pride.

Pride is more than simply being proud of something. If you do something well, it is acceptable to feel good and proud of yourself. However, pride sneaks in when you begin to see yourself as better than someone else or if you think that you are doing well because of your own efforts. This is why it is important for the servant to be humble. As you serve others, remember that your motivation is to give glory to God not to gain the credit for yourself.

Now that we've laid out the traits of a servant and two traits to avoid, reflect on your own heart. Do you portray the qualities of a servant throughout your day? Or, on the other extreme, do you struggle with slothfulness or pride? No matter where you find yourself in regard to the traits, remember that ultimately your priority must be to reflect Jesus–the perfect servant. We will never fully reach His example, but the Holy Spirit will continually work to sanctify us and make us more like Him if we put the effort into it as well.

Practical Ways to Serve

Now it's time to get real. We've been focusing on your motivation for service and some characteristics that you should reflect as you serve, but what does it look like to practically serve others? You're a college student, so you're busy all the time and have a million things constantly calling for your attention. How do you incorporate service into your busy life? We've got four suggestions that should help you get started.

The first way to serve is by serving sacrificially. This could look like donating money to a cause or giving up a Saturday afternoon to volunteer somewhere. Though it doesn't seem like you have a lot of free time or money, I promise you have time to donate a few dollars or even an hour or two of your time to a worthy cause. Ask your church if they have ministries that reach out to the community and see if you can volunteer to help. Serving will require you to sacrifice something, but if we're serving a Savior who literally sacrificed His life for us, it no longer seems like a burden but rather a joy.

The second way to serve is by serving anonymously. As mentioned before, one of the greatest enemies of service is pride, and when you find ways to serve when you know for a fact that you won't receive any credit, you're portraying humility. Look for little ways to help others even when they will never know it was you.

The third way to serve is by serving the unlovable. What we mean by this is that you serve people who are not easy to get along with. We all have those people in our life who, for whatever reason, we simply have trouble relating to. However, Jesus calls us to love our enemies and pray for those who persecute us (Matthew 5:44), so he leaves no exceptions. When you show your enemy that you love them by serving them even when they don't deserve it, you open the door for a gospel conversation in which you explain how your salvation has changed your perspective on how you serve others.

The fourth way, and the most important way, to serve is by using your gifts to serve the church. In the book of 1 Corinthians chapter 12, Paul compares the church to a human body, and he emphasizes the fact that all parts of the body are important to the whole. If one part is envious of another and not doing its own job, then the whole body suffers. The same is true in the church. As a student, you have a lot to offer the church, and the church will not reach its full potential without you. The Lord gives all of us specific gifts so that we can serve His church, and He wants us to use them. He calls us to use our passions to serve the church because he calls the church to serve the community around it. When you serve the church, you serve others.

Conclusion

Servanthood is the calling of all Christians because Jesus Himself came to earth to serve humanity. We are called to emulate Him, and that means we follow His example and serve others the way that He did. By modeling your service around the four traits of a servant—humility, intentionality, compassion, and flexibility—you will be well on your way to a life that reflects our Savior, the example of a Perfect Servant.

<u>Additional Resources</u>

Caring for One Another by Ed Welch
The Character of Leadership by Jeff Iorg
Celebration of Discipline by Richard Foster
Spiritual Disciplines for the Christian Life by Donald Whitney

FIVE

⟡⟡⟡

Handoff

"What you have heard from me in the presence
of many witnesses, commit to faithful men
who will be able to teach others also."
2 Timothy 2:2

The fifth and final, but certainly not least, letter of the CRASH acronym stands for "Handoff." Throughout this entire book, we've given you information to help you grow in Christ and better understand your faith. Those are great, important things that will make you a more devoted follower of Christ, but something we have also tried to highlight in each chapter is the importance of sharing what you have learned with others. We have called this chapter "Handoff" because we will be discussing what it looks like to take what you have learned and "hand it off" to others. Telling others about Jesus and what he has done for you is the most important thing you could ever do with your life, but you cannot just leave someone hanging after you share the gospel with them. If the person decides to accept Christ and follow Him, the next step is for them to receive discipleship.

"Discipleship" is a term thrown around in Christian circles all the time, but it is often left undefined. We know that Jesus had twelve disciples, but what made them disciples? And for that matter, what qualifications made Jesus a disciple-maker? Jesus was a disciple-maker because He invested in people so that they could know Him more intimately and deeply. His disciples were called that because they learned how to follow Him and because Jesus charged them to continue the cycle and to go out and share the gospel with others as well. The same definition of disciple applies to followers of Christ today. Every single follower of Christ qualifies as a disciple because we should be learning how to follow Christ and helping others follow Christ too. This chapter is designed to help you better understand discipleship so that you can grow as a disciple yourself.

The Goal of Discipleship

Before we can discuss the methods of discipleship, we must first look at the ultimate goal of discipleship. Paul describes this end goal in Ephesians 4:13-16:

> "...until we all reach unity in the faith and in the knowledge of God's Son, growing into maturity with a stature measured by Christ's fullness. Then we will no longer be little children, tossed by the waves and blown around by every wind of teaching, by human cunning with cleverness in the techniques of deceit. But speaking the truth in love, let us grow in every way into him who is the head --- Christ. From him the whole body, fitted and knit together by every supporting ligament, promotes the growth of the body for building up itself in love by the proper working of each individual part."

The goal of discipleship is to unify the church body and to help one another mature in our personal relationships with Christ. As we grow closer to Christ, we are less susceptible to be "tossed to and fro by the waves" and more likely to stand firm in our faith. Maturity in Christ results in confidence in faith–the two go hand in hand.

However, in order to grow in maturity in Christ, you must have discipleship. Discipleship is the process of getting to the end goal, and there is always room for discipleship no matter where you are in your relationship with Christ. You should always be receiving discipleship from other Christians, and you also have the responsibility to disciple others by teaching them what you learn about Christ and how they can know Him more as well. The discipleship process does not stop; discipleship is a cycle that duplicates and multiplies. Jesus Himself described the discipleship process in what we call The Great Commission in Matthew 28:19-20:

> "Go, therefore, and make disciples of all nations, baptizing them in the name of the Father and of the Son and of the Holy Spirit, teaching them to observe everything I have commanded you. And remember, I am with you always, to the end of the age."

Jesus tells His original disciples that they are to go teach others as well, prescribing the discipleship cycle from the moment of His ascension. This command continues to this day, and it applies to every one of us.

Key Components of Discipleship

If the end goal of discipleship is to unify the church body and to help one another mature in our personal relationships with

Christ, how do we practically do this? How do we disciple? The process of discipleship contains five components, each of which we will discuss in detail: Bible, Mission, Intentionality, Journey, and Relationship.

The first component of discipleship is the **Bible**. If you are going to grow in your relationship with Christ, it is logical to assume that you need to study God's Word. The Bible teaches us about God and His plan for salvation, and to effectively share the gospel with someone, you must know what the gospel is. Not only does the Bible teach us what the gospel is but reading and meditating on the Bible is vital to our sanctification process. This is why we have weaved various Bible verses throughout this book. We want you to know that this content does not only come from human minds, but from God's Word, our ultimate authority. In fact, the Bible itself speaks to how important it is to discipleship in 2 Timothy 3:16-17:

> "All Scripture is inspired by God and is profitable for teaching, for rebuking, for correcting, for training in righteousness, so that the man of God may be complete, equipped for every good work."

These verses reveal that all of Scripture, every book, chapter, and verse, is useful and important. We cannot neglect any part of the Bible because every word teaches us about God and how to become more like Him. Reading, meditating, memorizing, and teaching the Bible are all important aspects of discipleship because without the Bible, discipleship is impossible. Without God's Word, it is impossible to know God.

The second component to discipleship is **Mission**. Earlier in this chapter we looked at The Great Commission (Matthew 28:19-20), which explains what exactly our mission is until Jesus comes again. Our primary mission is to "make disciples" and we do this by going, baptizing, and teaching. We go to the lost and share the gospel with them, when they accept Christ the church baptizes them, and then we teach them more about God through His Word.

Not only does the Great Commission tell us how we are to make disciples, but it explains who we are to disciple as well. We are to make disciples of "all nations," meaning that no person of any ethnicity is excluded from the gospel. Every person on earth is worthy of salvation, and we must go to them and tell them about Jesus, so they have the opportunity to respond to Him. Evangelism is a vital part of the mission to make disciples because without it, new disciples cannot be made.

The third component of discipleship is **Intentionality**. It is easy to let people slip through the cracks, so discipleship requires an intentional plan of action. Jesus was intentional with his discipleship because He took strategic opportunities to teach them and He invited the disciples into His life. We are to mimic this strategy, bringing others into our lives and showing them through our own example how to follow Christ.

The following list includes some ways in which you can intentionally disciple others:

1. Form a small group of your friends and study the Bible together
2. Meet one-on-one with someone and study the Bible together
3. Do both fun things and mundane together where you can practically show them what it looks like to live like Christ in all life settings
4. Share a meal together and discuss how God is growing you.
5. Invite the person you are discipling to do chores with you and share you can glorify God through it.

The fourth component of discipleship is **Journey**. Salvation is a one-time event, but discipleship is a life-long process. We never outgrow our need for discipleship no matter how mature we are in Christ. We will always need someone to disciple us, and we are called to always be discipling others as well. Jesus' disciples stayed with him from the moment they were called until He ascended to be with the Father. Even after Jesus ascended, His disciples went around in groups and pairs because they could not do the work alone. While they were planting churches, they still needed discipleship themselves.

Not only is discipleship a lifelong journey, but it is a continuous cycle of multiplication. The memory verse for this chapter is 2 Timothy 2:2, and we chose this verse because it describes the journey of discipleship multiplication. When we come to know Christ, we must share with others and teach them so that they can then go tell others as well. It is an ongoing process, a chain that continues beyond what we could ever realize. However, this multiplication cannot happen if you do not initiate discipleship to begin with. If you are a follower of Christ, you are likely a part of someone's discipleship chain. It is up to you to keep that journey of multiplication going forward.

The fifth component of discipleship is **Relationship**. In chapter two, we discussed relationships in great detail because they are truly that important. For discipleship to occur, you must know the person, and that requires a relationship. These relationships can look a variety of ways. It could be a friendship, a mentor-mentee relationship, a pastor-church member relationship, or anything else you can think of. The exact nature of the relationship can vary, but it must be the sort of relationship where both parties know one another well.

No matter what your discipleship relationship looks like, the important thing to remember is this: You cannot be discipled alone. God designed us to be in relationship with others, and discipleship is no different. It is also important to remember that discipleship relationships must primarily come through the church. While your small groups and one-on-one relationships with your campus ministry are important, you should do your best to find community and a discipleship relationship from your church.

Who Should You Disciple?

Now that we've learned about why and how to disciple others, let's discuss who to disciple. We touched on this briefly in the previous section about relationships, but it is important to remember that discipleship requires effort from both the discipler and the one being discipled. If one party is more invested than the other, the relationship won't work. For this reason, we have come up with three qualifications for a discipleship candidate:

1. **Faithful**. The person must be willing to commit to meeting regularly and putting in their share of the effort.
2. **Available**. The person must be good at scheduling and managing time. This can be learned, but they must make time for discipleship into their lives and not consider it an afterthought.
3. **Teachable**. The person must be humble and willing to learn. Much of the discipleship process is reading and learning to study the Bible, and this requires work.

These qualities do not necessarily show up in a person right away, but they will become obvious as discipleship continues. If a person seems to be unresponsive and aloof no matter how much you try to reach out to them, that could be the Holy Spirit telling you to move to someone else, at least for the moment. If you pray for opportunities for discipleship, the Lord will provide them even if they don't look like what you originally imagined. However, if someone is unresponsive, you can continue to pray for them and for the Holy Spirit to move in their hearts. While not everyone is ready for deep discipleship, the Lord is still moving and will provide discipleship relationships for those willing and ready.

Conclusion

Discipleship is not only an important part of the Christian lifestyle, it is the Christian life. If you are a follower of Christ, you are responsible for discipling others and being discipled yourself. Jesus does not tell us it is an option, but rather He commands us to make disciples as we go about our lives. The ultimate goal of discipleship is to unify the church body and to help one another mature in our personal relationships with Christ, and our hope is that this chapter, as well as this book as a whole, has helped you understand the process of discipleship and why it is so important to the Christian life.

Haylee's Experience

My primary experience with discipleship has occurred through small group Bible studies. Through all of my four years of college, I was a part of my campus ministry's small group ministry in some format. As a freshman, I joined one, and it was a blessing to learn from girls who were older than me. They gave me good advice for how to navigate the many challenges of college, and after my freshman year, I knew that I wanted to lead a small group myself.

For the following three years of college, I led small groups of freshmen. It was a joy to meet and disciple girls younger than me like I had experienced myself. However, my most meaningful small group from college occurred when I was a junior, and The Lord led me to initiate a Bible study with my group of friends. For two years we meet weekly, going through various books of the Bible, and our time together grew us closer both to The Lord and to one another.

The primary thing I hope you learn from my experience is that discipleship is a "need", not a "want." Had I not attended those small groups, my relationship with the Lord would not be what it is today. Through those times of discipleship, I had a community that encouraged me to pursue the Lord, and we grew closer to one another as a result.

My one regret from my discipleship over the years is that I neglected the local church. I spent most of my time in my campus ministry, so I never truly found discipleship in the church. While campus ministries are great, they are no replacement for the local church. My encouragement to you is that you seek out the local church and make that your primary means of discipleship. Discipleship through your campus ministry is also important, but it cannot take precedence over the church.

Quintons Experience:

Growing up in the church, I had heard of the phrase "make disciples" but only when it was associated with the Great Commission. I was told it was a command in the Bible and that I should be doing it. There were a few times where I was told "how to make disciples" but it was always principles, which is good, but I still didn't know what it looked like.

Once I went to college, my BCM director began to actually disciple myself and one of my best friends. We met weekly to spend time in prayer for each other, went through a book, and a time of accountability. This was not the only way that we were discipled, however, he also took us to the store with him to see how he interacted with people on a normal basis and see what he did on a regular work schedule. He taught us how to follow Christ wholeheartedly, be a good servant and leader, as well as a good husband and father.

While serving in church, I also had a few men who would encourage and mentor me frequently. Each person shared different parts of their lives and what God was teaching them. They also opened their home to share what a godly family looks like while also seeing some struggles that may happen. Most importantly, they all taught me about who God is and that He wanted to use me in a unique way. I was challenged to obey God no matter what and to serve any way I could. I learned that discipleship was not a weekly meeting but a journey to become mature in Christ and to share with others what we had learned about Him.

Additional Resources:

Multiply by Francis Chan
Replicate by Robby Gallaty
Making Disciples by Gene Warr
The Cost of Discipleship by Deitrich Bonhoeffer
Discipleship that Fits by Bobby Harrington and Alex Absolom
Discipling by Mark Dever
Discipleship.org
Discipleshiplibrary.com
Disciplemakingtoolbox.com

SIX

⌒⦿⌒

Bringing it all Together

You made it! You successfully made it all the way through the CRASH Course. You have learned about Christianity, Relationships, Answers, Servant, and Handoff, and now we're going to take some time to reflect on the high points of each chapter.

The first chapter, Christianity, explains the narrative true story of the Bible and how God has worked throughout history to bring about His plan of salvation for the world. Our goal for that chapter was to give you an overview of the Christian faith because if you do not understand it, you cannot share it with others. Also, by providing you with a "big picture" sort of framework for the Bible, you can see how God's mission to redeem the world has stayed consistent through both the Old and New Testaments. From Adam and Eve's first sin to Jesus' death and resurrection, God has had a plan the entire time. That plan has always been centered around restoring God's relationship with humanity, and that brings us into the second chapter.

Chapter two, Relationships, describes the importance of relationships in the life of Christians. Our first relationship, and the most important one, is our relationship with God. That takes precedence over all other relationships, and our lives should reflect how we value Him. One way in which we demonstrate our love for God and our growing relationship with Him is through serving His church. The church is God's vessel for sharing the gospel with the world, so participation in the life of the church must be a priority no matter what stage of life you are in.

The third chapter, Answers, deals with difficult issues and questions that will arise as you share your faith with others. We focus specifically on the issues of salvation, suffering, and story because we believe that equipping you in these three areas will give you a great starting point to better understand your faith. The "salvation" section describes how you can have a relationship with Christ and how our salvation is unique to that of other faiths. In order for you to share the gospel with others, you must understand salvation because that is the message you are taking to the world. However, when you are telling others about your salvation, the question of evil and suffering will likely arise, and that is why we have dedicated a portion of the Answers chapter to suffering. The "suffering" section is designed to give an overview of the questions that you will face and give you a starting point to answer them. The third section of this chapter, "story," describes how you can use your personal testimony to share the gospel with others. While people can argue against the two other issues of this chapter, they cannot argue against your personal experience.

Chapters one through three focus on various facets of the Christian faith and how to understand it, but chapters four and five discuss how to put your faith into practice. Chapter four, Servant, explains how to be a servant like Christ. Jesus came to earth to serve others rather than to be served, and as Christians we must imitate Jesus as we go about our lives. This chapter describes Christ as the perfect servant and how His followers today can follow in His example and serve the world around us.

Chapter five, Handoff, describes the best way that we can serve others: discipling them. We can serve people all day with their physical needs, but if their spiritual needs continue unmet, we have actually done them a disservice. The first step to help someone become a follower of Christ is to evangelize and share the gospel with them, giving them a chance to respond and accept Christ as their Savior. However, it does not stop there because once they become a Christian, the next step is discipleship. Chapter five gives examples and guidance for how to disciple others and put what you learned in the previous chapters into practice.

It is important to remember that CRASH Course is meant as a basic guide to help you understand the Christian faith. As you mature in your relationship with Christ, you should continue to study and learn. This is a great tool to get you started and give you a framework for what the Christian life means and should look like, but you must take what you learned here and apply it as you move forward in your walk with Christ in the future as well.

With all that being said, we want to leave you with a word of encouragement and a charge. The Lord loves you. He desires to use you. He wants for you to know Him more and for you to grow deeper in your own love for Him. In fact, He loves you so much that He sent His Son to die and resurrect so that your relationship with Him could be restored. How amazing is that! It's a beautiful truth that is incomprehensible for our finite minds. You know this beautiful truth, and now it is your turn to go share it with others. Use the tools you've learned from CRASH Course, get involved in your local church and campus ministry, and go out into the world and tell others about Jesus!

RECOMMENDED RESOURCES LIST

Chapter 1
Biblical Theology by Nick Roark & Robert Cline
A Reader's Guide to the Bible by John Goldingay
The Old Testament by Richard Hess
The New Testament in Antiquity by Gary Burge, Lynn Cohick, and Gene Green
The Jesus Storybook Bible by Sally-Lloyd Jones (Yes it's a kids book but it's great so you should read it.)
The Baker Illustrated Bible Dictionary by Tremper Longman
Commentary sets that may be helpful: *Christ Centered Exposition, Wiersbe Exposition Commentary, Bible Speaks Today, New American Commentary, and The NIV Application Commentary.*
Ultimately, pick up your Bible and begin reading today!

Chapter 2
Concerning your relationship with God:
Knowing God by J.I. Packer
Something Needs to Change by David Platt
Abide in Christ by Andrew Murray
The Power of Knowing God by Tony Evans

Concerning your relationship with the church:
The Trellis and the Vine by Colin Marshall and Tony Payne
The Church Today by Paul Powell
Sojourners and Stranger: The Doctrine of the Church by Gregg Allison

Concerning your dating relationships:
Single, Dating, Engaged, Married by Ben Stuart
The New Rules for Love, Sex, and Dating by Andy Stanley
Boundaries in Dating by Henry Cloud and John Townsend
Things I Wish I'd Known Before We Got Married by Gary Chapman
Getting Ready for Marriage by Jim Burns and Doug Fields
The Meaning of Marriage by Timothy Keller

Chapter 3
Visual Theology by Tim Challies and Josh Byers
Christian Theology by Millard Erickson
Reformed Dogmatics by Herman Bavinck
The New Evidence that Demands a Verdict by Josh McDowell
The Cross of Christ by John Stott
Making Sense of God by Timothy Keller
The Reason for God by Timothy Keller
Evil and the Justice of God by N. T. Wright

Chapter 4
Caring for One Another by Ed Welch
The Character of Leadership by Jeff Iorg
Celebration of Discipline by Richard Foster
Spiritual Disciplines for the Christian Life by Donald Whitney

Chapter 5
Multiply by Francis Chan
Replicate by Robby Gallaty
Making Disciples by Gene Warr
The Cost of Discipleship by Deitrich Bonhoeffer
Discipleship that Fits by Bobby Harrington and Alex Absolom
Discipling by Mark Dever
Discipleship.org
Discipleshiplibrary.com
Disciplemakingtoolbox.com

END NOTES

1 Tozer, A. W. *The Pursuit of God.* Bloomington: Bethany House Publishers, 2013.

2 Grudem, Wayne. *Systematic Theology.* Grand Rapids: Zondervan, 1994.

3 Leeman, Jonathan. *Church Membership.* Wheaton: Crossway, 2012. The five things mentioned is a Southern Baptist view of the church.

4 "Your Story Is God's Story: Creating Your Testimony." Cru. https://www.cru.org/us/en/train-and-grow/share-the-gospel/evangelism-principles/how-to-tell-your-story-worksheet.html.

5 Calhoun, Adele. *Spiritual Disciplines Handbook.* Downers Grove: Intervarsity Press, 2015.

6 Murray, Andrew. *Humility.* Nashville: B&H Publishing Group, 2017.

Printed in the United States
By Bookmasters